Hope and Other Beautiful Things

Hope and Other Beautiful Things

Maverick L. Malone

—•TEMPEST PRESS•—

Cover design by Maverick L. Malone with the assistance of Wombo Dream
Published by Tempest Press | tempestpressbooks.com

ISBN: 979-8-9916777-1-4
Library of Congress Control Number: 2025943219

Printed in the United States of America
Tempest Press, Chattanooga, TN

Handcrafted with rebellion, reverence, and real magic

For the fireflies

When you have nothing else, have patience, have compassion.
When you have nothing else, *have hope.*

If it doesn't go according to plan, I plan to burn

We agree to meet first thing, when Sunday slips into Monday, before tomorrow has a chance to toil us away or tear us to shreds, to convene before bed and discuss, and plus, I have a lot to contend with. You know, research, hypotheses, thesis, and all that.

I hear the screen door slamming and there I am on the enclosed back porch, the artificial sacrificial light of a laptop with 35% battery already aglow on the edge. Small feet padding behind, I kiss tiny fingers, hands. Someone is up late because of the word *need*. I think of The Many Uppercase Reasons I do what I do. Why ALL CAPS SONGS and I meet so late at night in dreams. The future by the name of a flower has a number one chart topping single on that playlist. I sing it often. Both of us asked for change this time: more than loose, more than Lincoln, more than *more*.

I follow *more* into the woods behind my house. People deemed much more important than I are there, already writing words into the night, letting those paragraphs guide us like solar powered camping lanterns, Maglite flashlights with four D batteries, the latest iPhone model that can throw its glow ten feet in front of you. Then there's me, trailing behind with the unknown as my guide and a handful of fireflies in a mason jar hung from the notch on a stick, protected, held carefully out in front, stepping cautiously, one two three steps always disappearing. And still I go, trudging into the forest with everyone else; and when they get too far ahead, their shine much louder than mine, fed by the "right" kind of importance, fueled by the "right" kinds of eyes, *I will keep.*

The difference between a flashlight and a firefly is one is born of earth. Even when it dies, it cannot wait to return. There is an insatiable hunger for keeping, despite the hurt, despite the burn, despite the pain.

Some of us are flashlights. *Some of us are fireflies.*

And so, I keep. The light will remain, I will gather more fireflies, I will make a fire from the night and send smoke signals to the sky. If I'm destined to die on some hill, then let it be the one finally found after they smoke me out of that forest on fire from the blaze of my own words.

Let it be for change.
Let it be for fireflies.
Let it be for her.

That ~~one~~ *first* time
I published a rejection letter

Dear Maverick,

Thank you for entering our annual chapbook prize competition. Unfortunately, your manuscript did not win publication, but we appreciated the opportunity to read it. We always expect a high level of quality in these books, and this year's entries did not disappoint. 2,160 manuscripts were entered, and so many of them were so good.

Two thousand manuscripts submitted translates into roughly 40,000 individual poems that we've read over the last three months. Given the quantity of poems, and that many of them are already published, it's very difficult to consider them individually in this context. If you'd like to submit any of these individually at some point, please feel free, following the regular submissions guidelines—we won't mind reading anything again.

We also still have no idea which manuscript is yours, so if you'd like to enter a revised version next year, you're also free to do that. (I'm just trying to anticipate what are always common questions.) There were a great number of manuscripts that we would have been proud to publish—we simply chose the three that we loved the most.

Anyway, thank you again for entering the competition. I hope you enjoy the winners, and your subscription to *[our poetry publication.]*

Cheers,
Tim

Dear Reader,

This book began the same way as all my others: first as poems on the notes app of my phone, which then grew a garden in a word document. This one, specifically, was edited down to thirty-six handpicked poems from one such document arbitrarily titled "Hope and other beautiful things" and then submitted to a nationwide poetry chapbook contest in which the winners would receive publication and distribution to thousands of subscribers. It *would* have been massive exposure. It *would* have been a spotlight chance. It *would* have been a lifechanging event. It became none of that *because it was always destined to become so much more.*

After months of hoping a new door would open for the words I'd poured my heart into, I finally got an email. *THE* email. You know the one, I'm sure. The one that begins with "Thank you." Thank you, *but.* Thank you, *but unfortunately. That one.* The gut-wrenching one that, in a single swift curl of a palm, can crush a dream to dust...*if we let it.*

I won't lie. It stung. It was my first official rejection letter as a writer since embarking on this journey and going all in. That rejection letter had me staring at the question mark tattoo on my wrist and raising all kinds of thoughts about my "enoughness." Tim said I wasn't enough. The people judging this contest said I wasn't enough. My cruelest self of decades past saw her opportunity and came rushing to the surface, echoing their judgment: "Look at all the work you've done. You put your best out there and even now, *you are still not enough.*"

For a day, I believed them. For a day, I sat with that heaviness and questioned everything because nothing had yet happened for me even in the tiniest sense over the last few years. While other writers and poets in the community were seeing increased book sales, getting reviews and opportunities, or at least seeing social media growth, I was stagnant. The one book I had published so far was stagnant. My social media was stagnant. I was still being told no. I felt like I was shouting into the great, expansive nothingness and it was getting me nowhere.

I struggled that day. On top of the internal and personal struggles I had been feeling on a writer level, on a mother level, on a *human* level, I felt exhausted, stressed, depressed, disheartened, defeated, and invisible. My life was already overwhelming with what I was dealing with at the time and that letter pushed me over the edge. I felt the rush of those limiting beliefs and let the tears flow about everything, not just the rejection email. That email was a metaphor. It symbolized so much more. It was a mirror held up to my own face asking me, "So what are you gonna do about it?"

Apparently, I was going to cry some more. I slowly opened the door to the fridge, bent over the fruit bin, and sobbed into a carton of strawberries. Then came the words from a sweet, tinny voice across the room. There's nothing worse than your 5-year-old asking, "Mommy what's wrong?" and having to swallow your emotions in the moment, put on your big girl pants, and defeatedly whisper, "Nothing, baby. I'm fine."

I doubted my path, my purpose, my passion. I doubted if I'm making a difference at all. I doubted if anything would ever happen for me or if I'm destined to live the small, quiet life of a 9-to-5 divorced mother moonlighting as a writer, crying into a carton of strawberries. I rode that emotional wave, *and I rode it hard*. Even now, from pages and miles away, I can hear you. "Oh boo hoo! One rejection letter. Come talk to me when you get your 78th." But I'm a poet who is prone to magnified emotions and dramatics—what can I say? It's those "firsts," you know? *They matter.* And sometimes they cut deep.

The next day, in a moment of clarity, I heard another voice. This time, it was the one I'd been building for the past two years; the only one that can pull me out of that dark place: *my own*. She lifted me to my feet and gently told me ***to keep***. Keep going. Keep hoping. Keep believing. She told me that Tim is not the keeper of wisdom or truth, especially not mine. She said that there will always be people that tell us no. It's part of life and thank god it is *because it fosters growth*.

It became a lesson. It became expansion. It became the miracle of "what if." What if I published the book anyway? What if I added more poems and made it bigger? What if I began said book with Tim's rejection letter? *What if rejection became part of the message?* Really, it couldn't be more perfect. What better lesson of believing in our dreams and holding on to hope than tuning out the naysayers and doing the damn thing anyway?

This is not a "Screw you. No one tells me no" kind of motivation. This is not a salve for a bruised ego. This is not a tit for tat "Haha, I'll show them" sentiment. This is simply publishing the proof of hope. This is an example of keeping. This is not letting a beautiful message go to waste. This is hitting submit on something I poured so much of my soul into that I feel deserves to exist in all her fullness, in a world that desperately needs the message. ***This is believing in that message.***

I am grateful for the people that tell me no because it forces me to pivot. It strengthens my resolve and conviction. It builds a thicker skin, and it integrates the lesson. This is laying the foundation for that second, third, seventy-eighth time I may be told no. For a book all about hope, dreams and the many beautiful things that abound in this strange and backwards world, I see that *"no"* was only the beginning.

Rejection. Even you are beautiful. Thank you for the lesson. I will keep: the light, the hope, the beautiful things. They will continue to come, each one in their own time.

And Tim? If you're out there, thanks for the input, but I think I can take it from here.

Cheers,

Maverick J. Malone

████ Maverick,

Thank you ████████████████████████████
██
██████████████████████████ We █████████████
██
██████████████████████████████████
██
██
████████████████ are ██████████████████████
██
██
██
██████████

████████████████████████████████ so ████████
██
██
██████████████████████████████████ proud
█ we ████████████████ love ██████████████
████████ you ████████████████████████████
████████ and your ████████████ poetry ████████
██

████████████

█████

Table of Contents

GLW on the 111 1

The preponderance of moments this life hasn't lived but that
doesn't mean they don't exist 2

The Dream Poet 4

When the Moon Sings 6

The Five Most Beautiful 9

Starcatchers 11

Rise of the Mermaids 12

A32 14

Sand Pebble House 15

In the Spirit of Barbara 17

The Magic of Rain 21

Quantum Superposition 22

Boy, why are you crying? 23

Let It Be 25

Happy to Serve You 26

Just a Seashell?! 28

The Peace in the Piece 29

Open to Interpretation 30

Feeling Tense 31

A Season of Change and a Reason to Write 32

The Persistence and Perspective of Gypsophila 36

Green Noise 38

Flor·iss·ment..39

If at first you don't succeed (part I)...................................40

Change Seats (part II) 41

Untold 42

Art class from the point of a pen.......................................43

Wild Things go all kinds of places, but they always end up here....45

Late for Bed...47

Falling in love with the world is like this 48

I plant myself in a poem and she grows roots. Before long, I have
an entire grove 49

Because If It Does Not 51

Heard it in a Dream 53

Heritage...56

When can we do that again?! 57

Thought Bubbles You Can See...61

True friendship is pointing out each other's chin hairs....................62

This Came Out of Nowhere...63

In All Things 65

Master Potter..66

Are You Coming?..67

She is like a Walking Poem 69

Two full droppers administered before bed: 1 for the heart and 1
for the head 70

Thrifted 71

An ahem and an amen...72

When You Love A Poet..73

The Ghost in the Attic 75

Vesuvius, meet Venus..77

Orchestra of Earth 79

The Image Appears: A Portraiture Study in Color 80

How I imagine it's going 82

Riverways 83

The Floating Steps..84

The Queen escapes the provincial worker beasts, builds her own
hive this time and watches it bloom in B-E-A-U-T-Y 85

No Small Feat 86

The Dream Poet lives up to her name in a noun of the same 87

Spanish Lessons..88

Beneath the Bridge..90

An Invincible What If..94

An Eloise May Song...95

The Crack Between Realms 96

Things that Remind Me This Life is a Good One...............97

A Greenway Cliff Conversation...98

Visceral 100

This is a Universe based on Expansion 101

I Spy gets a Glow-Up.. 102

For those who never read the instructions........................ 103

As Told... 105

Goodnight 106

Now a little help for my friends, the ones I know and the ones I
haven't met.. 107

But what does it all mean? 109

Cadenza in the Rising Flame 112

Beautiful Pursuit 114

An Acceptance Speech on Behalf of the Full Moon 115

.

GLW on the 111

I never go looking for the magic
it just has a way of finding me
in an endless game of hide and seek
these simple bits of story
like the Queen T-shirt you wore
or the picture frame
hanging on the back of my apartment door
and a slow dance to "Golden Hour"
across the creaking wooden floor

somehow, it all showed up one day
impermanent permanence impressed upon me
paradoxically
like ink on skin and ink over pages
a story on me mirroring the story in me

as written in the stars
I wrote it in a notebook
these momentary apparitions
no more separate from dreams than the part of me
that knows only love in a hopeful heart

the beginning of a story always was my favorite part

The preponderance of moments this life hasn't lived but that doesn't mean they don't exist

Do you ever feel memories you haven't experienced in this lifetime? I'm talking the kind that ripple gently on the surface of your mind, like a live watercolor on parchment where the paint isn't yet dry and the sky is blushing gold and you have this... *this feeling* in your soul? It's hard even for a poet to describe, but I will try.

At work, I sit facing a large four pane window. From here, I can see the parking lot, the pink dogwood trees prematurely blooming, and the star of every clear morning's show—the sun and his light parading proudly through the office. When the rays hit just right, I get glimpses of images, some momentary reminiscence of perhaps another life. I've lived many, and though I have inklings of some of these, today's has the word *Grecian* surfacing.

I picture myself bathing mid-morning in a white room, wistfully staring out the window into the indescribable blue of the Aegean. She is so inviting, so calming, *I want to drown in her.* I hear the intermittent sounds of limbs moving around in the bathwater. My brown hair is piled on top of my head, adorned with fresh laurels and puffs of bougainvillea. There are small glass vials of lavender and rose oil and *this light, this light, this light,* floods the room in the softest shade. I am bathing in it, too.

The colors outside my office match this view: pastel pink, mauve, cornflower and powder blue, amber, ivory, gold. I don't know what this Greek version of me has planned for the day but it feels like decadent peace, reading, learning. It feels like soaking my mind in art, philosophy, music. It feels like crumbly feta, slick olives, and smooth elegance for breakfast. It feels like life is easy, simple, there is so much gratitude for *just existing*. It feels like so many layers have been stripped away without the distractions of modern day. It feels like my heart melting into a warm pool of fragrant orange blossom wax. It feels like little nectar sips of fulfillment and flaky phyllo dough satisfaction. It feels like the cells of my body are peonies opening their petals to drink in the sun's nourishment.

I take this memory and let the words gather where they may, sentences and phrases giving soliloquies of their day. I imagine the beginning of these speeches as if each letter has just been born, breathing slowly, like the rise and fall of a sleeping infant's chest; her tiny pink rosebud lips, little fingers and hands, everything peaceful and delicate. *It feels like a blessing.*

Though this place is nothing my present-day mind can recall, it is somewhere I've been once, somewhere my spirit must know of.

It feels like a message.
It feels like wisdom.
It feels like being chosen.

It feels like being kissed and held by the magic of a poem.

The Dream Poet

At sixteen I wrote:

"the dream poet
shapes stars from air
and swallows them whole
her poems are not written
but painted in colors
that stain the mind"

eighteen years later
I fire up that machine

I find...
I think...
I know...
I believe...

there's more to this than *just* imagination
it is never *just* a dream

it exists to exhibit what's possible...
and shows up when it wants to lead

A quick note...

The next poem you are about to read began like this: I sat down to drink coffee alone on the porch; heard "that broke my life into song" in my head; fell in love with this phrase; jotted it down; read pages of someone else's words; sipped my coffee; listened; noticed a single wisp of dandelion in the wind swirling past that sparked my own imagination; immediately wrote the following poem, "When the Moon Sings."

This is ultimately what I want to teach and inspire people to do: to make perspective from paper and hold on to it, to make connections, *to keep going.* Life is full of so many hard moments but they are often the ones that make us. Without struggle, without challenge, there is no change and no reflection.

I want to teach people how to make art from a single moment, how to find a poem from the tiny almost unnoticeable dandelion seed, to hear the music in the silence and to navigate the night simply by telling my story and making my art.

But there is no manual for this and no predetermined set of standard rules, so it makes that hard. It will be different for everyone but I hope that through my voice, I am an example of how hard moments and pain become passion and purpose.

It's like the 500 miles Clarissa Pinkola Estés talks about in the La Loba section of *Women Who Run With the Wolves.* You can't stop at 500 miles. It would be easier to stop there because we become so exhausted, so tired, and we think, "This is good enough. It's not Eden but there's water. It's not heaven, but there's a little less hurt."

Don't settle for only intermittent magic when it can become your life. It is the one who soldiers on for that 501st mile, that last push, that births the moon and lights up the darkest room. That returns water to the desert. That makes song from silence.

If I can go from a fragile, fragmented, fearful girl afraid to sing in a broken world, to this, a woman who roams wild with her wonder and turns everything to song and magic, wanting only to share that with the same world that once cracked her painfully and brutally open, *anyone can.*

That's the miracle, cracking open. Revealing what has been within you all along. But you have to be willing to try. You must be willing to travel through darkness to find it.

When the Moon Sings

I am sitting on the back porch overlooking the sandy creek, listening to the chirps of birds and crickets. My small dog pads across the floorboards in a skittering of paws. My feet rest on the brown rattan coffee table in a symphony of creaks. The coffee is cold and the coastal Florida air is slightly crisp, a kind of comforting morning chill carried on the wind when she blows through the slats in the railing and finds her way to my face, as if tilting my chin to say, "Follow your own advice. Look up."

The sky is peppered with long, skinny clouds like stretched dough. The moon is still out. Proud. A lone dandelion seed jetés past, turning through the air and escapes through the railing. Off into the distance of slash pines it goes. I wonder about the dandelion puff from which it came, if it was willingly separated, destined to become wish from some small child's imagination, or if it was ripped away unexpectedly and thrown into the hungry mouth of wind, searching for yet another soft place to land like the rest of us.

And there it follows, my mind, doing what she so often does, making connections, frantically gathering dots and drawing novel constellations among them, anointing each with a beautiful name: Remembrance, Hope, Perspective.

I am reminded of where I now sit, nestled among the quiet that sounds so different than what it once was: a cold, dead thing that could make even the snow want to leave, where only the tiniest pinpricks of light would every now and then find their way. Brief flashes of warmth as if to remind that there was something more but I had to learn how to listen first, how to turn my eyes into telescopes with string lights gathered from the fragments of myself I kept going back for.

I think about how many dandelion seeds make up the whole, how many it takes to comprise a person like me, how many wishes I made once upon a star that are now something of ladies-in-waiting to be rendered real when the timing aligns.

I think of the moon in broad daylight and the heat that fills my chest, the poems that flood my head, when I find myself suspended in a moment like this, turning the key on memory and reflection.

There is always something changing here, hope that feasts on connection no matter how small; on every kind of dream, every kind of thought.

Such music in the quiet now.
How miraculous. How magical

the silence

that broke my life into song.

The Five Most Beautiful

five
the crest of each wave culminating in thousands per second
how together as one they look like entire schools of fish
arching up and out of the water
breathing and undulating only momentarily
in shadows that play peek-a-boo with the sun

four
the way that same sun glitters on the surface of the ocean
in an interpretive dance of light that never speaks twice
every moment
a new song

three
how the sand looks like cinnamon sugar
tinted the softest and subtlest shade of lilac
in the early dusk

two
the silhouette of fifty seagulls against sky
as they glide along the horizon
enticing the other twenty-five perched on sand
to take off while some of the others return to land
another natural dance

one
the fullness and gratitude
ever-present here (she gestures outward)
and here (she points to her heart)
and the peace in the knowing
that love is never far

Starcatchers
for Lilly

out of gravity's pull
we are lifted up!
up!
up!
into the expansive unknown
starcatchers in the dark
we hunger for those pinpoints of brilliance
to build our fortress of stars
lit with the greatness of a million dreams
an expansive universe of wishes
we collect and preserve
protecting their delicate luminosity
from the dark hands of doubt
and the harsh realities of a world
so swollen with hate

and should these little lights dwindle
we will cradle them in our palms
and shape newborn dreams from the stardust
breathing life anew out of darkness

Rise of the Mermaids

you don't need to hold your breath anymore
let it out
you've been hidden underwater but you're surfacing now
an echo can still be heard
even twenty thousand leagues beneath the sea
something calling, luring, encouraging
intoxicating and melodious if you ask me

sip on that
each one unique pressed into sheet music of soul
your notes won't sound like anything this world has ever known
are you ready to pull it out?
can you let it go?
deep breath
now.

break rules like waves
remind everyone why you came
position your mouth against the pale cheek of sky
and leave a kiss, an energetic imprint
tell her what it is you wish
ask for wings
sing.

the high pitch like a dog whistle fills my ears
Pavlovian siren call
what does your dream sound like?
it is coming.

the inevitability is Aeolus and his breath
propelling a lost and weathered ship to shore
Atalanta hunting down stories, insatiable for more
Bastet prowling for your most powerful secrets
moving stealthily between shapeshifting scenes
a quiet shuffling
morphing into the low hum and rush of drums
Daedalus hammering
sparks flying
meticulously redesigning
liftoff
weightless

soar so close to the sun this time
he is burned by your own light
let it out
soar so close to the sun this time
you become him

A32

I will always pick the window seat, content
to stare for hours tucked into the bend of time

pondering the magnificence of the universe
stretching on in all directions

shapeshifting on a loop
transfigured and transformed

a vast field of snow one moment
an endless ocean of sky the next

puffs of clouds suspended in brilliant blue
like bobbing helium balloons

casting ink blots of thoughtful shadows
on the patchwork earth below

a breathtaking and bright reflection
of the luminescence of the soul

Sand Pebble House

from the water
the six-story beach condo at night looks like a dollhouse
I see lights on in some of the rooms
enough to glimpse silhouettes and shadows within
but the majority are dark
empty
forgotten

I see a person, maybe a woman,
standing at one of the windows
I wonder if she sees me

I imagine most of the occupants
are off with family this holiday weekend
and those that remain are vacationers
or vagabond wanderers
like myself
those too who have escaped to the coastline
perhaps in search of riches
the kind we can only find within ourselves

I see this building lit up and wonder
who else might be in there right now
thinking, dreaming, wanting

who might be laughing and dancing
who might be crying
who might be surrounded by others
who might be alone
who might be sharing a bed
and still feel a chasm of separation

I spin around in the water to face the vast blackness of night
both of us now turned towards what lies beyond
both of us waiting and believing
both of us refusing to give up on the North star
and the hope and healing
born from the tiniest drop of a single dream

and I can already tell from the way she is lingering
both of us
filled with enough love
to overflow the ocean in between

The following poem was compiled unexpectedly (as many of mine often are). I was sitting in a café, organizing this manuscript when I began overhearing snippets of conversation from the group of older women at the table next to me. They had a deck of tarot cards on the table and apparently gathered annually to pull cards for the new year as an act of faith and good fortune. A beautiful ritual.

"In the spirit of Barbara," I heard one of the women say, as she opened the deck. My ears soon began selectively picking up bits of their conversation, which I quickly typed for safekeeping, to follow where they would later lead me. The quoted italics below are pieces of that conversation that fluidly and effortlessly wove a poem from my fingers. I have no idea who Barbara is (or was), but I suspect she had something to do with all of this.

This one is for her and for those women. Thank you, for your unexpected magic.

In the Spirit of Barbara

Late afternoon and I finally
haul my laptop and writing materials from house to car
make my way downtown to the Uncommon place
I come to sometimes because it's quiet
can hear myself think, ya know?

except today it's slightly more challenging
says eyes here (screen), hands here (keys)
ears torn between
the big band and bells on the stereo blaring post-Christmas music
and the table of three older women chattering
over two o'clock tarot in the middle of the coffee shop
their hum a little louder
than the thump of drums backing soaring vocals
still, I settle
still, I hear it

"In the spirit of Barbara"
the deck taken from its protective box
the women brewing
a little magic at the coffee shop, holding court
this annual meeting to pull cards for the new year
traditions among friends, among souls

I don't look, too obvious—just listen
imagine the cards are angelic and gilded
lightweight, shiny foil squares
the Sistine in a wise palm that knows much of love
but believes there is always more to learn

"This is such a wonderful game of chance"
that unmistakable shuffle
the reverence of quiet connection
sacred intention setting

"What do I need to hear?"
the opening line cast
far into some otherworldly majestic realm
Go Fish for stars

A card for artistry:
"...part that really speaks to me is the bird of creativity.
I can be so scattered right now in my creativity
because there's this thing in my head
of you better do this and that and this. I want to slow down
and focus on different media one at a time."
"I truly believe everyone is an artist. It's just been squelched out of us."

A card for light:
"I don't know what to do with it, but I love it."
"You want to be it."

A card for believing:
"This is something I need—faith"
"A new guitar and a new keyboard to teach myself music—
faith that I'll be able to feel it."

I think
what magic, what chance
why I chose this café of all options
what brought me here
what brings us anywhere

the closing remarks of the group cut through
the last dregs of coffee gone cold at the bottom of my paper cup
illuminates the lifecycle of a poem that has become chapel:

"We are all getting what we need."
"You have to let it go."
"Did you know she wrote a song about it?"

Indeed.
She did.

The Magic of Rain

right as rain
the rippling reflection of violet and magenta crepe myrtle trees
in sepia pools and puddles on concrete
an inverted memory made tangible in her whisper
liquid sagacity on skin sinking in
a bedtime story of hushed spirit
a thrush of benevolent songs
fine-tuned along the hoods of cars and pavement
the congregation of crystal dewdrops
resting on pews of verdant grass, clover, ferns
illuminating the sanctitude of their purity
the compassionate way
such rain brings a serene surrender
asks only for your ears
your eyes
your heart
a cleansing of every shard of sorrow
every grain of grief
a reprieve
a hope
a healing
write as rain

Quantum Superposition

they said it wasn't possible
to be in two places at once
but how do you explain
the body summed up in geography
and the little corners we've carved out
while the heart breathes superimposed
over places we yearn to go
and the head makes a home among clouds?

Boy, why are you crying?

When they ask, *"Why am I crying at this?"* I encourage it.

I applaud the loudest for the highly sensitives, the emotional creatives, the clash and boom storm-music soloists, the turning blood and guts to gold artists, the daringly and radically different, the tender neurodivergents, the believing in the unseen and speaking it into existence ageless children, the feeling the richness of all your feelings feelers.

So yes, my god my god, cry and keep crying. Spotlight that noticing with your firefly spark, your candle glow, your lighthouse beacon. *Cry at absolutely everything.*

Cry at the orchestra of sunrises and flowers tilted towards sky. Cry at first kisses and last goodbyes. Cry at the various stages of stars— shining, fading, falling. Cry at the symbolism of the moon in the epic of night. Cry at how impossibly beautiful and deeply tragic life is. Cry at the simplicities you have been gifted: breath, language, love.

Cry at the limping goose with the broken leg trying to catch up to the rest of the flock. Cry at the tiny brown moth whose life you saved when you carefully caught him in your bathroom and released him unharmed back into the wild. Cry at the three little girls in a line holding hands hiking the gravel path, toddling behind their mother like wide eyed ducklings. Cry at the enormity of every small thing because it's reflective—so too are you the patina aged copper pennies of long-awaited monumental change.

Cry because you value all creatures, the hierarchy erased.
Cry because you know only love and will never understand hate.
Cry because you still feel hope even when drowning in despair.
Cry because you repeatedly choose to be caring, generous and kind.
Cry because you see beauty where others avert their eyes.

Cry because there were too many times you couldn't. Cry because you're finally allowing yourself to. Cry because you know healing is not weakness. Cry because you're human.

Cry because this life is making meaning out of you.

Let It Be

everyone speaks to being on top of the world
but have you seen it from the bottom?

let it be from bare earth, eyes cast towards Orion and the Little Dipper
from the sidewalk pointing out globed planets in an attempt
to discern Jupiter from Mars billions of burning miles away
from curiouser and curiouser rabbit hole mazes
deep beneath cracks in concrete opening into the antithesis of tunnel vision
from ground zero of the rubble of your smoldering past
from the billowing future hoisted from the mast
that knows how to harness the high seas of left and write at last

from the half sipped horizon of black caffeinated candor in a cup
from the hidden majesty beneath zebra striped iris petals
folded over in a love drunk sigh
from the shade of the singing Canary and Phoenix palms
in a silhouette kiss of sky
from the persistent resilient shoreline and her relentless restless waves
from beach grass meadows and vast painted desert spaces
with more than enough room to roam
from new foundations formed
from your own beautiful body that finally feels like home

we climb and scale and rush and run
just to reach the apex from the bluff
so savor those bold beginnings from the bottom
let the journey be enough

Happy to Serve You

what is it that draws us into ourselves? and what extracts us?
the hustling morning whistles for my attention
and we are suddenly swept in a rush
the comb as it moves feverishly,
gathering my daughter's hair into a ponytail
the lunchbox packed fat and happy with cheese and apple slices
the shoes shoved onto feet and the overpowering mint slicked over teeth
the brown wool sweater with its woven image
of a blue and white coffee cup pulled onto my body
a familiar frustration, a comfortable itch

what is it we carry day in and day out?
tides washing up unto ourselves
moon-blistered and night-bristled by the unrelinquished hope
that morning might reveal what is it we missed
while we tarried too long and forgot
to flip the eggs, burnt the toast
busying ourselves on the inside of a "what if" world

despite my refusal and penchant for absentmindedness
I am dumped like the contents of my bag
the keys I can never find, the crumpled receipts I keep
the extra straws and napkins I grab
never really knowing why;
I never asked

another Monday slips into the chair opposite me at the table
notes the exposed chaos without commentary
sips the same coffee I can't seem to cut out of my life
a necessary ritual, simple magic
she is soft spoken in that regard

she tries, she tries
a head nod, a you there, a quiet and kind reminder
counted out like coins, patina prayers
metallic minutiae of persistent wishes
what is the ordinary offering me?

a long pause—
and will I take it?

Just a Seashell?!
for Shell – IYKYK ;)

how dare you!
she is the sateen concavity of calcareous exoskeletons!
a crescendo of tide pool melodies from harmonious waves!
Neptune's mixed media for painted summer shores!
crustacean safe haven in violent uproars of thundering savage storms!
glittering trinkets and glowing treasures from loving Mother Earth!
sacred omens and beautiful blessings bedazzled in the sand
emerging and disappearing at will with Poseidon's sleight of hand!
a playful symphony of spiraled scallops in a butterflied beach parade!
a mulluscan metaphorical ode to the first chapter of a name!
no, she is *never* a mere seashell;
do not refer to her as such!
and never, ever in conjunction
with such a word as *just*!

The Peace in the Piece

I wake up and go walking along the canyon I call home
all day I am gone
picking desert marigolds and reading by the river
learning to exhale like the wind
holding the panorama of my life within this skin
that only ever wanted to be held
in the same way the heavens
can cradle both the sun and moon at once
so easily balancing the scales of sky

it is here
I am swept up in the sanctity of earth and air
and when I return
the sunset tucks me in the four poster bed
of an early evening awash in cinnamon and amber
that yields to the unfolding infinite onyx night
sparking in a show of celestial flair
like tiny lamplighters in the dark

and though the hour is no longer golden
I shall remain so
and so
I shall remain

Open to Interpretation

days stacked in lucid translucence
translucent orange blossom honey
honeyed Florida sunshine
sunshine in a square of garden
gardens blooming thistle thoughts
thought of you when I wrote this

this might seem like disjointed incidence
simply speaking
but go on
I dare you to digest the significance

go on
I dare you to find its meaning

Feeling Tense

"I'm feeling a little tense today," she said.

"I went to bed in the past
and woke up in the present
but I'm still dreaming of the future."

A Season of Change and a Reason to Write

a cloud stops by and I get on
because I am curious where she will carry me
she asks me
"if you could go anywhere right now, anywhere at all,
do anything, anything at all,
where would it be?
what would it be like?"

I settle into her fluffy silver and blue puffs
pulling them closer around my body like a down comforter
and bury myself in a dream
she leads me to a beach where the sun is just beginning to sing
in a spectacle of soft orange and amber
dancing and sparkling across blue and purple waves
a familiar feeling for a familiar day: warm but not hot
the kind of warmth that permeates every vein and every organ
like a slow gentle melt from the inside

here
a group of us are having brunch on the beach
everyone's seated on multicolored cushions
gathered around a low lace-covered mahogany table
with silver domed platters and mismatched china
toile porcelain and silver and brass spoons and forks
among flower petals scattered like confetti

I smell the food before I even see it: butter, honey, cinnamon
towers of stacked biscuits in a pool of blueberry preserves
warm banana brioche French toast

sparkling cider pouring into coupes
slices of crusty baguette heaped with spiced eggs
the golden yolk gently pooling out

I take my seat at the head of the table
nestled against a stack of vintage pink and white striped hat boxes
I open the largest one and crown myself:
a fascinator made from an impressionist painting
seafoam, peach, pale pink and powder blue
a pastoral scene where roses and birds all hum a different tune
in a crescendo of a promising spring
this place I'm trying to reach

the brushstrokes give way to velvet
give way to silk
give way to satin in a spiraling flock of origami birds
taking flight from the foundation of paint

as I clip it to the side of my amethyst hair
my dress changes: lilac chiffon draped sleeves
and fabric flowing down past my feet
the whole thing covered in a hundred tiny purple lilies

I feel like Monet if he were his own painting
I feel like the cloud I rode in on
I feel like a rusty chest that waited patiently for decades
at the bottom of the sea until it was finally found
a million rubies and sapphires all spilling out
I feel like an emerald-skinned mermaid surfacing for the first time
I feel like the rainbow ombre shine and silver sheen of an oil slick
I feel like the satisfying final line of a stanza

I gently tug at one of the birds from my hat and pluck it from the others
she rests gently in my palm, motionless
I kiss each of her wings and whisper a prayer over her beak

she begins to breathe
she beats her wings and takes off
flitting around the other guests who begin to don their hats
each one shaped from my own mind:
the caramel fedora dripping with streaks of melted chocolate
anointed with a four-foot single owl feather;
the wide brim hat covered in pink fur
two tiny rhinestone cat ears poised on the top
and a magenta racoon tail cascading down the back;
fascinators of verdant green and peacock blue
overflowing with deep plum and magenta ostrich feathers
and strands of ribbon; a top hat
made entirely of gingerbread with pink and white frosting;
an oversized lemon rose splattered with pastel paint
a tiny nest of orange and pink canaries peeking from the petals

we clink our glasses
and I make a toast as I eat the same:
a perfectly browned slice of warm, thick sourdough,
slathered in honey
I take a bite and it tastes like imagination
six flavors melting together in harmony all at once;
something that looks sweet but tastes savory
before changing back to sweet

the slice becomes cake
indulgent chocolate with raspberry sauce,
garnished with mint
resting upon the plate
I take another bite and savor it
feeling the velvet caress my tongue
like the hopeful moments filling my head
like the love flooding my heart

I raise my glass in a salute to sky
grateful that little cloud stopped by
"to the dreamers," I say, tears welling in my eyes,
"you have always been my why."

The Persistence and Perspective of Gypsophila

The farmhouse table is strewn with dried flowers: baby's breath, lavender, and buttercup ranunculus bundled in glass vases. Quicksand roses the color of well-loved paper spilling over the top of the antique typewriter. Scattered scarlet petals and loose leaves awaiting the artist to arrange them onto canvas or into frames, to be married with sketches and faces and figures. To be transfigured, transformed. To be reborn.

You ask why I keep *"dead flowers,"* stating they are not beautiful. And in that moment, I realize how vastly different our perspectives are. I am astonished that one could look at a pressed daisy or a dried bundle and not marvel at her wonder; how she was once an elegant bouquet for a bride, an uplifting gift of hope for a grieving loved one, an affectionate display of thoughtfulness and acknowledgment in a single stem.

The beauty in a dried flower lies not in the once vibrant brilliance of her hue or her fragrant scent; not her ample blooms or her burgeoning petals presented in a show for sun; not her lively dance of dewy morning kisses or the way she plays maestro to a host of buzzing bees and chirping birds with the orchestration of her unfolding petals.

The magnificence of the *dead flower* is that her beauty, her elegance, her grace and splendor are all perfectly preserved—that she is not dead at all. She is very much alive: immortal, in fact. She is poetry, emotion, and wisdom encapsulated as a singular moment in time.

You may look at the faded hue of her smile and see a decaying thing. *I* look at her faded hue and still see her as she once existed. I look at her and listen.

The miracle of the dried flower is that she asks simply to be loved, not only for what she once was, but even more so for what she has become.

Green Noise

It was bound to happen eventually
you had to break the house in somehow
you knew this was coming
you've been here before
the bathroom floor and deep breaths over radio silence
now every pothos and succulent knows
the familiar sting of stomach pins and needles
the process of how butterflies become blisters
making the shower scald feel like a caress
oh, but listen and lean in a little closer
let me tell you a secret all the wise ones know
sometimes it gets worse before it gets better
but the best part is
it always does
get better, I mean
because grief
it cannot survive in a body like yours for long
light always finds a way
and if you're patient,
the rain will even teach you to dance

Flor·iss·ment

Noun:
a never-before-seen word now in existence / a novel rendition of
an inventive definition / a floral arrangement of singing gratitude /
an outpouring; an overflow / born only from the flourishing mind
/ of one mad hatter poet / a herd, a school where each mammal or
fish / moves harmoniously in unison / overwhelming love that
dawns upon oneself / like the most breathtaking sunrise /
experienced for the first time / awestruck appreciation for a
person, place or thing / as heart songs spinning pain into gold /
what happens when truth acts as witness / and every broken piece
/ finds its place within the whole

.

If at first you don't succeed (part I)

7 what if life can be distilled by saying
11 it's a paint by numbers game
9 blank shapes filled with colors of our
6 choosing until the image renders itself
2 complete and sometimes we pick hopscotch
12 instead of cereal box
10 make a mess, move outside the confined
6 borders provided
3 each finger joining cracked pepper with
3 whisper, summer peach with pine forest
9 fossil becomes riverbend
11 changing course where we fall
4 in love with the stars because we've
6 mastered backstroke, shavasana, astronomy
10 *look up*
5 notice how night makes the skin glow
1 a series of choosing
7 creating in service to the soul
12 trial and error and fudging the rules
12 out of order becomes backwards book
8 a line a circle an ending a beginning
3 my hands flipping open every paint pot
11 enamored with the sound of the lid
6 snapping open closed open pop
6 pinky dip drop smear streak dot dot
12 paint dollop claiming the territory of my fingerprint
3 calling itself mine just as I keep rearranging the shades
2 searching for the one without a name
1 who will write my own across the top

Change Seats (part II)

12 paint dollop claiming the territory of my fingerprint
3 calling itself mine just as I keep rearranging the shades
12 out of order becomes backwards book
11 changing course where we fall
12 trial and error and fudging the rules
3 my hands flipping open every paint pot
6 pinky dip drop smear streak dot dot
6 snapping open closed open pop
11 enamored with the sound of the lid
9 blank shapes filled with colors of our
6 choosing until the image renders itself
3 whisper, summer peach with pine forest
9 fossil becomes riverbend
3 each finger joining cracked pepper with
6 borders provided
10 make a mess, move outside the confined
2 searching for the one without a name
1 who will write my own across the top
8 a line a circle an ending a beginning
5 notice how night makes the skin glow
2 complete and sometimes we pick hopscotch
12 instead of cereal box
11 it's a paint by numbers game
1 a series of choosing
7 creating in service to the soul
4 in love with the stars because we've
6 mastered backstroke, shavasana, astronomy
7 what if life can be distilled by saying
10 *look up*

Untold

there is a bottleneck of stories just clamoring to get out

I can sense them
roaring, snarling, slinking, trumpeting,
flapping, squawking, stamping, bleating,
bellowing, growling, laughing, howling

for now
I will feed them bare-handed between the bars of the cage
these morsels and bits of magic that I've made

for now
I will keep persistently tinkering and toiling away
forging freedom's key for their inevitable escape

soon
I will grant them all asylum on the page

Art class from the point of a pen

It's iconic, isn't it? Van Gogh's Starry Night of soul, a thousand swirling lights burning up through his body, exposing the divine.

It makes an impression for a reason. He created something beautiful from an asylum, from such a tortuous, dark place and isn't that the most human thing there is? To persevere through the pain and paint the night and take the calloused and bloodied red and turn it into diaphanous boundless blue? To pluck stars like guitar strings and make them sing? It makes you think, we're all in some sort of asylum here, aren't we?

Some are still there, some have escaped, and some are just now learning to shape the key with paint but if Van Gogh can turn *that* into *this* then maybe we can look a little harder within to find out what our own starry night is, to do the bravest thing we can think of, and to me…that is to believe.

To believe that the asylum can become sanctuary, can transform into the luminosity of svelte moon-glow soft to the touch and infinite planetary brilliance in present moments strung like freshwater pearls from words that have ceased to seethe and burn but have become cool melted mercury, quicksilver tongues no longer collecting dust, sharpened by unyieldingly patient trust, carving windows from the steel cages that imprisoned us.

A vision is a precious commodity, a rapturous rarity, a beauty to behold and when it is birthed from the expansive universe of a wild mind that is not afraid to go there, the best thing to do here is share and share alike so that a single starry night can go forth and multiply as blissfully brighter days; so that pain is no longer the currency exchanged; so that paint on canvas can exist in every kind of shade; so that love, hope, and truth are the famished flames that consume and the asylum's forever changed.

What is a starry night if not an honest, awestruck poem painted from our deepest pain?

Are you willing to get messy? Can you be covered in that paint?

Van Gogh made it famous…*but it is you that makes it brave.*

Wild Things go all kinds of places, but they always end up here

a Wild Fantastic
yes, I've mentioned this place before
so step inside (the rhyme is fine)
if you want to hear some more

such an imaginative sphere
there in the back pocket of mind like a pool table
(if it were a water bed)
fluidity and flow
waiting for your shoot-and-strike next big move

those who wander here do not feast of fear
only love working from the inside out
outer space inversion
topsy turvy creativity coercion one cannot control
to paint, to sing, to dance is the natural rhythm
(the only one we know)

think a shimmering silver assemblage
that grows hungry for love that lasts
think Eden think Elysium
think every wonder of the world contained
in a maze of copper catacombs

the discovery *is* the game
and the latest craze is called *questioning*
is called *noticing*
is called *waiting*

draw the medicine from your brain
the spiraled tangled mass of words
of visions of ideas
like birds of prey out on the prowl

look out now!
to catch you must be quick!
you must *allow, allow, allow.*

Late for Bed

I read at the riverbank until the sun goes down,
tucked in for the night but I
am still not tired. My wilder parts want
to swallow dawn but it's much too far down
from here and besides I have a dog to let out,
so for now I linger, leaving pieces of me behind
on these rocks; skipping poems like worn stones
into the evening waves. I gather
my things and eventually make the hike
back to the parking lot; drive the thirty minutes home;
unlock the door; greet the dog;
run the bath.

I relax and allow:
thoughts, reflection, memories;
dab the rose oil on my hips,
place a few drops on my wrists,
climb into bed with Pablo and Plath—
I can never choose just one.

They coerce
my eyes to flutter closed but my mind and I
wander awestruck and faith filled—
we are still not tired.

There is too much life to be lived.
There is too much love to be given.

Falling in love with the world is like this
after "Breaking Trance" by Mark Nepo

feeling the breeze through the open bathroom window
as it kisses my wet skin; I kiss back
a displaced but familiar scent
hiking the middle of a forest in the Pacific Northwest
watching a sunset from a rooftop deck in sweat pants and wool socks
moss that feels springy underfoot
dark mint chocolate melting on my tongue
the slow bubbling caramelization of marshmallows on a rotating stick
beach stargazing and painting your face in the sky
the many forms of flame: bonfires, birthday candles, passion
waking up to a chilly cabin room when I'm covered in flannel and a quilt
museums with floor to ceiling masterpieces
and benches positioned in front of frescos
napping in an apple orchard at the turning point of fall
saying goodbye, leaving for eleven days, and feeling
the all-encompassing warmth of missing someone from 2,133 miles away
the welcome home embrace
gratitude for the many ways I've changed
feeding feelings to attentive ears
peeling oranges and sucking the juice from each slice
one hand softly reaching for another's
hearts connecting
love filling every crevice of this life

I plant myself in a poem and she grows roots. Before long, I have an entire grove

Seek the sacred.

She is there, hiding in plain sight waiting for you to arrive. At morning's first light, she is there, lovingly wiping the sleep from your eyes and handing you her own, a glistening lens of rainbow fractal prisms in which to view the world.

This kind of perspective has the magical ability to transform: everything is a lesson, everything is a metaphor, everything is a simile exactly like the one hanging from your lips in a good morning kiss. Mornings are the highest caliber of sanctity. This is the most important meal of the day for the mind, where she can so easily reflect and rewind, without being too shrouded in ominous London fog. Mornings are half-drunk caramel-colored cups of coffee with a trail of scattered cinnamon already making shapes and stories along the inside of the rim: a horizon of spotted mountains, a stippled crescent moon, a secret language told entirely in constellations. Mornings are warming thoughts of someone's image materializing in your head, how so easily you can conjure their eyes or their heart or their scent. Mornings are bowlfuls of freshly washed berries with an indulgent dollop of whipped cream and a shower of sprinkles because *why not celebrate a Monday?*

In the mid-afternoon, treat it as if it were a flashing yellow stoplight and a Children At Play sign: *slow.* We so eagerly wish to escape the cage of the day and before we know it, she is gone in a flash. A disappearing act you can never get back, when afternoons are the very definition of magic. Afternoons can be many colors besides golden and in fact, even the drab gray and black ones are some of the most wondrous. Think of rain on a roof, think of thunder outside illuminating the storm within you. There is beauty there too. Think of a sky in the brightest shade of blue. Think of picnic blankets on grass and reading beneath a tree and the spirit softening to new possibilities. Think of the view from the top of the parking garage. Think of pick-me-up lattes and hot buttered croissants. Afternoons are surprise texts and the anticipation of waiting for a face and an embrace. Afternoons are the parade before nightfall's Broadway play.

Oh, and isn't she a show, indeed! In the early evening, remove your shoes and dip your toes into the gentle flow of cool water in the creek. Catch the sunlight bowing to the earth as she stretches her rays like arms through an audience of oaks. Listen as the curtain of night goes up and the performance begins with every cicada crooning and each speckled frog croaking. Evenings are pure poetry to which my own could never rival. Evenings are soul revival at the church of shower steam. Evenings are cups of aromatic hibiscus tea. Evenings are a hundred good feelings moving through every small moment of intimacy, especially every time we hold hands just to make sure there is something still there to hold on to. Evenings are practicing my words aloud and imbuing every sound with intentional emotion that stands out, proof that magic abounds, that *the sacred is always around*.

I lead with my voice. The throat knows the way.
And if I can't carry a tune in a bucket, I'll put a poem in its place.

Because If It Does Not

does it not make your mind writhe and spiral and sing?
does it not elevate you to places you've never been?
does it not lead you into the forest, encouraging you to get lost?
does it not quietly cradle the parts of you that hurt the most?
does it not burn you in the best way?
does it not pump you full of purpose?
does it not say your name like a sacred incantation?
does it not spill the very contents of your cognition
just to see the mess it makes on the floor?
does it not send you running to define unfamiliar words
like you're feeding a nest of baby birds, hungering
for grammar and punctuation?
does it not shove you into a time machine
and mash buttons on the keypad,
content not to know the destination?
does it not punch holes in your flesh like a sieve
and let the grief seep out?
does it not run its fingers through that sorrow
and turn it into the Mona Lisa?
does it not hold a megaphone to your ear like a call to prayer?
does it not light the pyre of every old version of yourself
ready and willing to commit such arson?
does it not dive into the cobalt abyss and still manage
to emerge with gems each time?
does it not magnetize beings to your message,
longing to be soothed by the sounds
cresting quietly over alliterated scintillated syllables?
does it not connect, reveal, burn, heal, alchemize, theorize,
aggrandize, expand, contract, breathe and bleed?

does it not taste like plump and ripened infinity?
does it not reflect to you your own all-encompassing divinity?
does it not illuminate the verities of humanity
in the boldest, most mysterious way?
does it not brew a cathartic and medicinal tonic
from letters steeped in questions of why you came?
does it not remind you just how much you were always
absolutely
irrefutably
positively whole?

then friend,
it simply isn't true writing
if it does not feed your soul

Heard it in a Dream

The opposite of Parseltongue is Flowermouth, and I am fluent.
It is the utterance of goodness, where every word
is nectared sustenance and bees buzz eternal
in a heart-dance heady hum. Press your ear to the petal
and she'll kiss you in a whisper. Noise is what happens
in the background when you aren't paying attention,
but *sound* is what wakes us up and draws us toward ourselves.
Can you listen closer?

Love is its own language, yes, but Flowermouth
is something else entirely. It is the ability to draw you near
with only a glance, turn silt to gold, ash to rose,
despair to hope. It is how I speak when spoken to,
even more so when no one's listening,
sing when flying solo, alchemize every kind of stubborn pain,
conjure change from a groggy dream.
Allow me to explain.

In Flowermouth, *angeline* is a word that is both noun and adjective,
used interchangeably, meaning "innocent artist."
Not ange*lic* like "exceptionally kind or sweet"
but say it with me—*an-gel-ine*. In Greek,
it means messenger of God, but I prefer…
messenger of truth, of heart, of beginnings.
Perhaps you reject that portion entirely, "*god*,"
it is not important but at least worth the mention.
After all, the Greeks were very wise,

but the definition to which I will now describe
refers to a similar kind of kindness, innocence, purity.
Not in a religious sense. No not at all,
but an artistic one.

You see, all artists are messengers.

When we speak and say, "They are angeline,"
we mean they are a painter of soul, a music maker
of their innermost messages with the purest of intentions,
a curator of ethereal cognition and a powerful voice for change.
Their art does not come *from* but *through*.
As above, so below, they are a receptacle for truth
and it pools and pours and spills.

Angeline is swearing allegiance to your soul,
ferociously committing to your own growth,
diving headfirst into the mysterious depths of the unknown.
Angeline, absolved of shame and guilt for they have shed it many times,
an honest and just student of humanity who chose life
to consider its complexity and unearth a deeper meaning.
Decided to do just that—teach, sing, paint,
proclaim of all that they have found,
of all that they have learned.
To feed the throngs of thrashing hungry baby birds
whose minds have not yet hatched,
whose hearts do not yet know kindness.
To invite and invoke.
To find and share joy.
To plant genesis in a poem.

Love, release the old stories from your ribs,
and let the sun hold you open.
Let it grow you.

Let it pour from your piano, your paintbrush, your pen.
Catalogue every new memorable experience,
every wonderful thing you will ever love.
Become a seasoned scholar of Flowermouth,
evergreen and angeline in perpetuity.

Gatherer of hope and other beautiful things,
bearer of the light your spirit brings,
songbird of the wonder your voice sings
you, your hallowed highness,
are the precise messenger this world needs.

Heritage
for my ancestors

the miniature Jewish prayer book, worn and weathered
from the refuge of his back pocket
all those long nights spent in a war that wasn't concerned
with the love he left back home
sent letters instead
with the fringe satin pillow cover
she placed at the coveted center of the bed
letting his memory, his words
hold her when his arms could not

the porcelain geisha with the broken hand
the painted paper fans
trinkets of far off lands she longed to go
a miniature violet vase in a Versailles scene
an amber glass elephant with his trunk proudly in the air
a Viennese dish with two waltzing lovers
she loved to surround herself with beautiful things
as I do now with the picture of her youth
encased in sterling silver
sitting tandem with her treasures

their memories have faded through the years
faces harder to recall
the corners furling with sepia tones blurring
and the lines of their smiles a little less defined
but the feeling lingers
the stories remain true
effortless and ever-present
the love
eternally coming through

When can we do that again?!

I read a meme today that said
"Due to personal reasons, I will not be reincarnating on earth again"
and I laughed and said with conviction
"Oh, I absolutely will!"

so I offer you this:

be in love with life
be in love with turning everything into an adventure
making tea becomes a countertop lecture
on the contemplation of mass-produced wisdom printed on a sachet
going for a walk becomes a hunt for leaves in the shape of hearts
and flowers that hold encyclopedias of knowledge
even the 9 to 5 grind becomes a NASA countdown
until you can rocket out of those doors and into waiting arms

be in love with laughing
until it physically hurts in the most beautiful way
with smiling even through the rain
with crying at some point every single day
to let everything you've been holding in finally escape

be in love with the luminous moon in her darkest night
the searing sun at his brightest and boldest
and the way they need each other to make sense
be in love with the words that come
when you have waited an entire week for them to show up
when it only took ten minutes of quiet and stillness
to open those floodgates and be swept away

be in love with learning the hard way
be in love with the shape of your changing body
dancing naked through the house
while eating handfuls of popcorn straight from the bag
be in love with showering to music at full blast
be in love with simplicity:
phones in airplane mode
spending all day doing nothing
the unmistakable, intoxicating smell of books

be in love with change and risk
be in love with hope
be in love with new perspective

be in love with the way a dress gently caresses every curve
and be in love with acceptance when it doesn't
be in love with brightening someone's day
with witnessing their growth
with the changing definition of "home"
with the art of letting go
be in love with the kind words from friends when your world
feels like it's coming to a burning, abrupt end
be in love with the concept of phoenixes
of fire
of birth
of death
be in love with transcendence
be in love with how a single phone call or a text
can so easily reestablish connection

be in love with winter:
the crispness of morning and the crackling fireplace
the patterns made from frost on windowpanes
the emanating warmth from an extended embrace
after weeks of not seeing their face
be in love with the death in all things
before new life can take its place

be in love with the intensity of every sense:
velvet palms clasped tight
soft kisses in painted moonlight
fragrant blossoms singing at your bedside
be in love with those same flowers long after they have died
be in love with crying
be in love with exhales and sighing
be in love with the process of refreshing
redlining
redefining

be in love with fireflies coming alive at dusk
be in love with a smile lighting you up
be in love with the pause you are offered every time you feel stuck
be in love with thunderstorms and the lessons revealed in rain
be in love with water in every form
for cleansing such deeply rooted pain
be in love with the way 4:00 pm light looks
coming through the blinds of a one room beach efficiency
and the sand that inevitably finds its way into everything:

between each toe even though
you rinsed them clean before coming inside
sprinkled along the bedsheets
clinging desperately to every article of clothing
refusing to be shaken
be in love with that sand and its stubborn determination

fall in love over and over and over again
with life
with things
with people
with places

let every granule of that love come through
don't brush it away

keep falling in love with you

Thought Bubbles You Can See

I like to write poems
love letters to no one, really
on the backs of paint chips at the hardware store
tucked in the title pages of bestsellers
front and center
on the coveted main entrance table
scrawl quotes on little slips of paper
left haphazardly around town
affirmations on post-its
stuck to sleek glass reflections
and lipstick outline smiles
when you just need one to borrow
graffiti hearts and grand slam truth
on the inside stall doors of gas station bathrooms
doodle caricature cartoons
filling every inch of cardstock squares
rewrite the lucky lotto numbers on fortune cookie slips
exclamation marks on extra-large tips
conjure some simple magic
when the earliest part of a day
so soon
begins to rip
and the only thing left to hold on to
is knowing somewhere, a kind stranger
is holding on to you

True friendship is pointing out each other's chin hairs

Is mentioning that one elusive piece of spinach between her teeth when she smiles that no one else was brave enough to; is texting at midnight to make sure her flight safely landed; is gathering emergency contacts and addresses when she solo travels; is offering the coveted final bite of sticky toffee pudding; is singing Wannabe down every Backstreet; is saying "that's what she said" and erupting in fits of laughter because she actually did, in fact, say it; is paying her way with no expectation in exchange only for her joy; is encouraging the tears over everything: starfish, sunsets, men; is texting her from upstairs that you need a ten minute hug; is hiking together far ahead of the rest; is giving constructive feedback and honest opinions; is name dropping her in a podcast; is writing her a poem; is reaching out when *mother* becomes too nuanced and difficult; is *sisterhood* through supporting, through encouraging, through connecting over the humanness of it all.

This Came Out of Nowhere

waking up the muse is a quiet stirring
a subtle whirring of hummingbird wings
defying gravity in the concavity of carnivorous minds
Venus fly traps of a different kind
slow motion shut-ins as I run from room to room
opening every window in this house
with its one floorboard that continually creaks
refusing to remain silent
this seam ripper across stitched lips spilling blue ink
from an exploding pen of thoughts chewed on too much
like bitten half-moon fingernails pressed
into old hands made new again
tracing and replacing the dinosaur DOS programming
that just couldn't compute anymore
as if certain identities were always
planned obsolescence

the heart becomes the cipher of an ancient hieroglyphic spirit
gulping secrets down slow just to rewrite their stories
freed from a gilded sarcophagus
that was only ever good for gazing
feeding the eyes rather than the mind
shades the endings in brilliant acrylics
instead of hand-me-down grays
and all those parts that couldn't stay
dissolve into pixelated punctuation

carried off by the contour of a copper ingenue
who sits at her typewriter at the back of my brain
and pushes the phrase of the day up through my throat
just to watch the inner mechanics I can't see
light up like a pinball machine ping ping pinging
all the right words in effortless timing
senseless until
the hour is ten steps in the past and patience
transfigures confusion
to clarity
at last

In All Things

I used to think love only a summer's day
        a romcom
        a Louisville slugger
        battin' a thousand home runs
        what the fairytales
                said it was

but this too—is *this* not also *that?*
        to be madly in love with the world

                and the world

      w h i s p e r s   back

Master Potter

You are different and I like that
you hold perspective like wet clay on the wheel
and it whirs round and round
your fingers lightly trailing lines
the mass taking shape

you lean in, make it say something
make it sing

sometimes that something collapses
and there you go
whirring it round again

Are You Coming?

there are numerous ways
to get to the places you've been trying to go
for a reeeeeeeeeeeeeeeeeeeeeeeally long time
and don't you think maybe now
you owe it to yourself to try?

keep going

there are moments you don't know yet
like safe passage as you fumble your way
across a train trestle in a tornado
...on roller skates
...*blindfolded*

but if you pull the light from your chest
wrap your worth up in words
and tie it taught to the tail end of a rogue wild thought
you can sail all the way down
where the track ends and possibility begins
carried off far away from this place
on a song and a thousand stories
because *that's* ingenuity
that's vulnerability and visibility
bravery and beauty
that's transforming the mechanics of your mind
into a first class flight
to see what's been patiently waiting for you
just there on the other side

so ignore the railroad ties
that seem to fall from the sky
and let your god or mine
climb inside your obtuse mind
and be ready
when both of them show up at the same time
with cans of hairspray
…and a lighter
(I bet you can imagine what comes next)

you see
people like us
were never waiting on a train
because the places we're going
could never be reached by following tracks

we were always destined
to forge our own path

She is like a Walking Poem

stay with me, here, she says,
stay with me as I drown in rushing rivers
of letters that destroy and create
in the lightning storm of inspiration
that strikes way more than twice
and the softest touch of sensual syllables
with a slow-motion caress in lullaby breath

allow me to feed you canary yellow
how she is tart at times and others
a frothing wave of smooth clotted cream riding an ocean of tongue
borrow these brown eyes and try them on so you can see
the entire universe on the opalescent interior of a single seashell
her trumpeting uniqueness of striations
and lyrical lines like rays of sun
or the Renoir in a rose and the Monet in a marigold
how the streaks of color sing in operatic harmony
and oh! the atlas inscribed on my palms
the worlds they have seen and the tales they have told

allow these words to find you
hold them, do not crush them
stay with me and open
let me be your walking poem

Two full droppers administered before bed:
1 for the heart and 1 for the head

I drop in, I root down; reaching through dirt and crust; anchored in love; a holy connection between two heavenly bodies: stardust flesh and eternal earth; from this space I see what I need, what calls to me through divinely guided vibration and energetic frequency; protected, held, safe, seen.

I feel the words and savor each one as I speak:
uncharted waters of open conversation; eyes looking *at* instead of *through*; morning light pooling in the room; two caramel macchiatos between friends from a tangerine sky at 7:00 am;

bare feet on damp grass; the language of butterflies; a child's tiny hand clasping your own; a tinny voice whispering, *"Mama"*; rose petal and lavender bubble baths by candlelight; the amber glow of two Himalayan salt lamps; incense with scents of "courage" "patience" and "surrender"; soft instrumental music on the stereo;

gentle stretching; cups of steaming kava tea with a touch too much turmeric; a familiar smile; chewing on the next chapter of a lighthearted novel; one hand resting on a snoring dog's back as you sleep;

keeping the towering oak doors of your heart propped open; watching every bit of dazzling light swell; poem after poem, all written as exquisite spells.

Yes, there you are. All is well.

Thrifted

There is magic in the discarded
bliss in simple things when second sight is swallowed
as heart, as home, as feeling
I wonder how many lives these boots have lived
the places these suede stilettos have been
who has worn that floral satin robe and what they might have seen
I think of the many bodies it may have caressed
whose skin was sacred, whose was solely flesh
whose was riddled with torment

I think of the oil painting with the cottage
like the one I've seen in my own mind
amidst a dense forest that laughs in light
shakes her branches gently, says, "come, child"
I think of the walls this frame has graced:
a grandmother's living room as she knits
an entryway with the perfect view of guests over for a visit
a bedroom with a comforter in a polka dot print

I ask the waxy plastic plants
if the light feels silken on their leaves
if they also love being sung to
if they have heard the tale of the velveteen rabbit
if they too know how real they are
because of the joy they bring

I hear the answer as a tinkling bell: *yes*

An ahem and an amen

you are the blinding mess god made
when she rolled the sun along her palms
split passion and fire in two
sliced like a beautiful piece of ripened fruit
with the saber of her own intention

squeezed every last bit of you to pulp and rind
and then birthed you anew into the soaking dawn

now when you open your mouth, she says
the sun will spill out and the world
will have no choice but to drink

When You Love A Poet

when you love a poet
she will sing you to sleep with her words
and wake you in the kind of lyrical gaze
that sparks magic under your skin
she loves hard and feels things so deeply
that it generates its own kind of heat
and speaks in magnetic soliloquy

her thoughts rhyme sometimes
and she will never tire of describing
the way your eyes look in the moonlight
or how your touch is like Orpheus
leading her back from the dead
resurrected in your song and lured into bed

a poet will cherish your love
and wear it in an amulet around her neck
just to feel the infinity between two bodies
at any moment
the sheer thought of you
evoking euphoria like watercolors
bleeding into being
and words endlessly spilling
from the place where inspiration
makes love to passion

because a poet knows
we
are more than carbon
more than skin and breath and bones

that we
are daydreams on repeat wrapped in silk sheets
and open hearts that can see in the dark

that we
are really just creation
imitating art

The Ghost in the Attic

I lived in a haunted house for a long time
blackout curtains drawn, windows painted shut
no stranger to luna moths and the pallid glow of moon
through curtains thick with dust

I lived in the library
slept on a bed of books
shoved far too many things in an art box attic
I locked every other room except those two
and always avoided the hall of mirrors

I hung a single painting above the mantel—
Gustav Klimt's *The Kiss*
it was a strange and faint remembrance
a flickering past life premonition
a reminder my story wasn't finished

I built a fire as questions wandered in
began burning away the cobwebs:
what is it like to be loved that much?
what is it like to be held in that way?
what is it like to recognize the right thing and learn to stay?
what is it like to expose your shadows to someone else's light?
what is it like to not hold your breath all the time?
what is it like to have a soft place to land?
what is it like to exist exactly as you are?
what is it like to love in high definition instead of from afar?
what is it like to receive just as much as you give?

what is it like to unlock, to release, to open from within?
what is it like to live inside *The Kiss*?

plot twist
I can't share the rest of this
not yet

August is still a work in progress
and even I
don't know how it will end

Vesuvius, meet Venus

The heart and mind work in tandem now. The heart,
with her voracious appetite for adventure, beauty, love;
she who only wants to feel and breathe and be. The mind
with her constant curiosity now spoon-feeds honeyed ideas
to the insatiable heart: a nibble of mountain, a bit of canyon,
a bite of coastline.

Maybe we could go, she suggests.
Maybe we can make this work.

The heart never thinks twice.
She just does as she pleases, knowing the rewards
far exceed any risk. The mind, though inquisitive as she is,
sometimes broods and bubbles entirely too much,
lingering and simmering on a shore of ideas.
She wants nothing more than to dive
into beaming oceans at sunrise, dance naked
beneath the singing stars, bury herself
in the outstretched arms of a beach,
but there are times even she cannot fathom such freedom.

Too burned by the hot eye of past,
too calloused by the gritty mouth of grief,
too weathered by the relentless downpour of pain.
She learned it was not safe to love or take or want,
and withdrew into her rough sketches and unfinished drawings,
content to rest in the rogue renderings of imagination
for just a little while longer.

But Venus makes her home among the most resilient of hearts
and knows only those handfuls of exact words
that so beautifully fit into each ventricle:
want, take, love.

Such a goddess within an eternal abode
never leaves the Vesuvius mind to smolder alone.
Born of sea, she keeps coming back for every part of me.
And for her, I would drown endlessly.
For her, the adventure of love beckons eternally.

Orchestra of Earth

the Moon married Night in a ceremony of silver light
fawning all over the silent Serengeti plains
as that scorched earth began to rouse and wake
dirt churned from the percussion of hooves
herds of stargazing gazelles
exuberant elephants rampaging on parade
trumpeters with trunks poised beneath the sky in praise
a baritone bellow of each lion's pride
the rushing woodwinds of birds with wings spread wide
every music note falling in glory on high
from every agape uproarious mouth
on the rapturous eve
the earth gave birth to sound

The Image Appears: A Portraiture Study in Color

The Dalí exhibit is a strange one but what did I expect
I too echo the sentiment when
the darkroom technique of my story develops
slow in the room's shadowed red

watch as I summon the soul through the camera lens
it is a simple matter of positioning you see?
both of us contrapposto closer to paper
we both know how to bear such weight by now, don't we?

our undoing renders this magic
the chemicals in us turning to fluorescent ink
intentional unparalleled heartspeak
uninhabited fragments of nature
untamable elemental forces

we appear not *in* but *as*
Palermo, Italy and the boundless Tyrrhenian
the heat of touch conjured from
brilliant Mediterranean light
free diving in the deep to gather meaning
to kiss purpose on the mouth
to experience the exhilaration and ecstasy
of getting lost among our many sounds

here we rent a small seaside house
move hall to hall and room to room
coming alive at night in all our strange
without the heavy constraint of time

we are sweet blue violets in a moon portrait
fencing, wrestling with the sun by morning
that same persistence of memory enshrining

both of us on film
in letters
as light

ah, here it comes!
a dreamworld developing now in full spectrum color
from what was only black and white

How I imagine it's going
for Jared

I hope that your phone died, or
got lost in a rogue wave, or
that you're skirting the edge of all reason
coasting careless down the interstate

I hope that you ghosted everyone again
because you chased the sunset instead
disappeared into burning amber, searching
for pieces of peace buried under sand

I hope that you're writing poetry by the glow
of a waning moon scanning the shore for gold
and penning possibility the palest tinge of pink
from the inside of shells washed along the shore

I hope that wherever you've escaped to
carved out from some grand master plan
that you're feeding your camera roll
with sunrises and silhouettes of sandpipers
seeing your spirit through *that* lens, noticing
your own brilliance on film in snippets and snapshots
recognizing how your resilience is always growing stronger
and enjoying the solitude
for just a little while longer

Riverways

there's a poem in my backyard and she is sinuous
like the soft mouth of the Beauclair River
wandering and winding into the wild
beyond the parted lips of a hopeful horizon
with a herd of lavender clouds galloping fiercely along her lines

her cattail arms announce to the sky in adoration
"this! come dance with me!
I am but life and breath and simple beauty
and you are born of the same!"

she speaks in baritone croaks and curious chirps
and the crackle of campfire
she has many faces that shift and change
but always adorned in a dress of spectacular Spanish moss
and when the night arrives for his rendezvous
I hang around late for that romance
I am swept away in the rush of their love
how the firework fronds of her palms gently brush against stars
trailing soft touch along raven skin of sky

I marvel at their effortless intimacy
how they can simply be
without even trying
reveling in the few hours they share
before her river parts ways again
and he disappears into daylight

I read her love letter again and again
my heart sighs
there's a poem in my backyard
and my god, she is wise

The Floating Steps

climbing **stairs**
autocorrects again:
stars that I scale; I am in
awe of those alluring stars;
they reveal presence all around;
that god or whatever you call her
is there, next to cleanliness
where you left her; wiped pristine
in the mirror of the bathroom; in the
adventures on the bookshelf in the
bedroom; tangled in cotton sheets
and sweaty bodies; in the efficiency of
every organ; in the calliope music
twinkling from the carousel; in the
painted peeling face of a wooden
horse; in the way a small child
climbs a tree again after falling,
back in the saddle of courage and bravery;
in her view from the bottom before
she can see beyond the canopy;
I am climbing
and the stars remind me
softly whispering
with each step,
you
are not alone;
you
are not alone.

The Queen escapes the provincial worker beasts, builds her own hive this time and watches it bloom in B-E-A-U-T-Y

The word is: pulchritudinous

Can I please have the definition?

Beautiful, attractive

Origin?

From the Latin word "pulchritudo" meaning "beauty."

May I have it in a sentence?

When she emerged from the dressing room in a floor length gown, she found her reflection to be quite pulchritudinous.

Pulchritudinous: tears, rain, tempest—
every word synonymous with falling water
the earliest part of morning when a dewy dahlia
takes her first sip of sun; the black and yellow abdomen
and diaphanous wings of royalty ruling entire kingdoms of leaves
blending colors and creating new shades of possibility
using the red pen to underline what still needs work
the first sentence of a new chapter
the Never Ending Story of metaphors
harmony between the roaring lion and the purring calico
the witch finally emerging from the wardrobe
clothes in a heap on the floor
bodies at rest
two tandem heartbeats
becoming
peace
pulchritudinous

No Small Feat

Let the adventure begin. And maybe that adventure isn't hiking the Himalayas. Maybe it's not an international flight. Maybe it's not sipping expensive red wine at a Roman cafe and catching the eye of some attractive stranger.

Maybe it's pushing publish or hitting send. Maybe it's applying for the job, the opportunity. Maybe it's just applying yourself.

Maybe it's buying a gallon of purple paint and redoing your living room in mostly Frida Kahlo decor or having an adorably kitschy all-pink kitchen, choosing maximalism when everyone else wants beige and gray.

Maybe it's randomly one day signing up for a class: a workout, a craft, business, language, expanding your knowledge on something you didn't think you'd ever try.

Maybe it's recognizing that change is needed. Maybe it's moving in, out, on. Maybe it's leaving or maybe it's staying. Maybe your greatest adventure is really just sayin' yes to what scares you the most.

Because what scares us the most will change us.
What scares us the most, in the end will save us.

The Dream Poet lives up to her name in a noun of the same

give me your downtrodden
give me your diminished
give me your underdogs
give me your overworked and your overlooked
give me your starving minds and your yearning hearts
give me your smallness and your scarcity
seed it all with tiny drops of love
just to watch it grow

give me your broken faithless belief
and see how quickly
it turns to hope

let me show you
how to stitch a dream back to its soul

Spanish Lessons

Ahorita is ambiguous Spanish for immediately.
right away. swiftly. urgently.
but also
in a short while. it won't be long.
soon, maybe later.
but if not now, then when?

I am cutting into its sumptuous sections with a pastry knife
my name inlaid ornate there on the silver handle
plating the beautiful two as separate
ahora—a tiered cake of now
ita—a dainty slice of little
a *little now*. a tiny moment.
a small piece of present tense
to have and to hold
to savor all that is:

consider the cornflower, bucolic blue in a field of sprawl
outnumbered yet makes its home in a ritual of ease
consider mouse whiskers with specks of snow up close
her tiny paws grasping the prize of shining seed
consider the language of intuitive hands along piano keys
paper, spine, skin—what do they say when they sing?
consider the dollop of dream that becomes epoch
a bashful hello leading to the heart thump fanfare of *I love you*
consider the dirt under fingernails
gifts from the garden as we go
turning earth upside down

making chasms from soil to peer into holes
to plant to pull to weed to exhume
consider the music of kettle whistle, paw skitter, baby laugh, breath
notes charted between ancient stars that reach our ears in an instant

consider this *little now*
in her *very*, in her *delicate*,
in her *shhh, wait* I think I hear it
cheek brush, eyelash bat, palm kiss
the fire crackle and harp pluck where feelings first arise
the small space of plentiful patient *this*
moving downstream as a single leaf
humble as they come, an epic ivy climb into the rush of day
doing what it does

we shape hummingbird wings from it
something so fast we slow the speed of sound
deconstruct *flight* into *float*
our diverse iridescence makes the mark here
looks ahead, arms outstretched
the coming of dawn, covering us

when I say I am learning Spanish,
this is what I mean

Beneath the Bridge

It is the day after Tax Day and our offices are closed, so I have the day to myself. I think about the fact that it is a warm Wednesday in April, the middle of the workweek, the middle of spring, and I am lying here in a middle of my own, on the grass getting stoned just as March predicted; taking bites of a coconut passion fruit donut and staring up at the canopy of dancing leaves, noticing how the lower branches of one tree shake in the wind while the taller tree has branches of steel.

I think about it as a metaphor. I think about how I make everything mean something. I think about how my melted to-go cup of ice water became poem inception, how the water inspired a poem, that was inspired by another I wrote over a year ago. I think about my feet tingling on the cool, bare earth. I think about the words *grounding* and *grounded*. I think about the concept of loneliness, how she is siblings with solitude, that much wiser sister.

I think about thoughts, passing like a flotilla of ships on a shimmering sea of those same late April leaves. I think about the many places I do my real work: in nature, cafes, Piano Man's bed. I think about the beautiful gilded cage I spend majority of my time and its keepers that sign my checks. I think about the colossus of whatever comes next.

I savor the moments, chewing slowly on the experience. I wanted this experience. This one I created. This moment in time lived by a version of me that will never exist again beyond the lines of this poem.

This carving of something that will never again be experienced the same way.

And then my thoughts quip, jokingly, "You don't so much care about the experience. *You just want to write about it.*"

I laugh to myself out loud, hearing this inner snark, with such a twinge of truth. I think about being that woman in a park, more relaxed than high, laughing to herself quietly and wondering who might pass by and smile at me, knowingly. Who might pass by and leave their judgment at the edge of my blanket for me to either pick up or leave behind. Who might pass by and wonder what I do for a living that I can feast of sun and ink in the middle of a Wednesday afternoon.

I wonder if years from now when I'm well-traveled and more established, if I'll think back to this exact moment before the Colossus Next, this seemingly ordinary and mundane middle (save for the getting baked part), and remember how I was so hungry for her life, for *her;* if I'll remember the chilly shade, the shape of my crumpled cactus tote bag and fringe jacket resting in the corner of the picnic blanket, the poem melting in the plastic cup from rays of springtime sun.

I wonder if I'll remember the earlier part of this day when Piano Man and I held hands and stared intently and lovingly at each other from across the table while two girls in the same cafe side-eyed us; if I'll remember the taste of his kiss, the tickle of his tawny temporary stress-grown 'stache, the four extra kisses and a last lingering hug goodbye on the street corner of Eighth and Chestnut that no doubt once again made him late.

I wonder if I'll remember how I so consciously felt the jiggle of my own thighs as I walked; how I momentarily cried from gratitude, knowing some future version of me is praising these thighs, this body, wishing she had it back; how the walk to my car became a trek through a jungle, the two women far ahead as fierce Amazonians jogging side by side with a jaguar between them; how that same walk was also a walk through a witch's house at the edge of the woods; how my brain doesn't even need any kind of mind altering substance to access this place because these are things I imagine naturally, daily, and immortalize in words.

I wonder if I'll remember how I stopped and retraced my steps back to the hole shaped like an ear in the sidewalk; how I bet it has heard lifetimes of secrets, bits of conversation, grand proclamations of love; how I stopped on a nearby bench to continue writing, even though I was already running behind and the next time the lightning struck, I kept walking and typing, like Belle wandering through town with her nose in a book; how I crossed the street barely looking up, willing the cars to stop because I could not; how I will always be late on behalf of the words and have a tendency to make others late from the size of my own love and a final lingering goodbye hug.

I wonder if I'll remember the peace I felt from it all: his arms, the sun, the doing nothing, these specific middle moments that make us.

I wonder if years from now, I'll reach into the back drawer of my mind, pull this album out and flip through its songs slowly, trying on my white fringe jacket to see if it still fits and touching my thick wavy purple hair, the curve of my growing thighs with the dimples of cellulite beginning to show, the faint trace of smiles etched into my face.

I wonder when the day will come
when *she* misses *me*.

I hope
it is a Wednesday in April.

An Invincible What If

There will be things sent to scare you, shake you.
Let hope be the loudest voice. Let hope be the only voice.
And what if all of it's a test? A gloriously F'ed up test
sent to see just how much you can hold?
How much you have grown? How far you're willing to go?

It gets a little bit easier each time, doesn't it?
Weathering the world? Bearing weight?
It's a couch to 20k, you've gotta let your legs build muscle.
You've gotta learn to stay in the lane you know is yours
because it was designed this way, *for* you, not *to* you.

What if every other thing just wants you to fail
because you're here to do something epic? Something great?
What then if you believe yourself nothing more than prey?
The world would be missing out! What a terrible tragedy!
Coming all this way only to stop when you're almost there.

What if your love becomes so big, you become invincible?
What if it becomes so big, you change the world with it?

Can I tell you a secret?
You're almost there. I've seen it.

An Eloise May Song

the poems stacked fat on the blanket
black ink among colorful emerald grass and picnic stripes
brown leather sandals placed neatly at the foot
laughter in the wind bouncing through branches
joie de vivre positioning herself gracefully
just so

the sun tilts his head forward to glimpse and gulp it down
a cup of water perspiring nervous in the noonday
but keeping its
cool liquid now
time in crystalline minutes melting between worn digits
getting on in age
warmed from the rays of persistent sun

a cup of water sings of a day well spent
the parched lips curling over the lid
wondering
where time went

The Crack Between Realms

Pyramus
here
outside
among the trees the rocks the river
earth and dirt and birds:

"A part of me doesn't want to leave.
A part of me is rooted in this peace.
A part of me wants to remain."

Thisbe
there
the other side:

"Because a part of you is a part of this.
A part of you is the same."

Things that Remind Me This Life is a Good One

Early morning sunlight coming through the window.
A slow drive over the inlet with marsh as far as the eye can see.
Gentle heat on my skin after so many weeks of winter.
Hiking by myself down Maritime trail and climbing a tree.
Exploring secret swamp nooks on Lagoon trail.
Spending hours without cell reception.
Gathering an abundance of scallops and shell fragments.
Eating gingerbread muffins and reading a novel on the beach.
Finding a poem in the sky.
Dining alfresco alone overlooking the marsh.
Water with lemon from a mason jar.
A three-course feast: feta and balsamic fried green tomatoes,
mahi tacos with a squeeze of lime, and peanut butter pie to go.
Being in good company because I know
I am the good company.
Burning a Sicilian orange blossom candle and listening to music.
Painting paper squares gold and filling them with poetry.
Reading in bed.
Texting sweet, romantic things
back and forth in French and Italian.
Your face as the last thing I think of before I fall asleep.

A Greenway Cliff Conversation

Him: Hey! Didn't you see the sign? No trespassing.

Her: Yes, I saw it. But my curiosity is infinitely greater than my obedience.

Him: You can't be here. Those cliffs are steep. I'm gonna have to ask you to come back on this side of the railing.

Her: No thanks. I think I'll stay here. Would you like to join me?

Him: What?

Her: Would you. Like to. Join me.

Him: I'm on the clock.

Her: I'm on the cliffs.

Him: You're not making any sense. You ok?

Her: Better than most, actually. But to some I appear worse. Depends on your perspective and what you're projecting.

Him: Look, I just don't want you to get hurt. It's dangerous over there. You could fall and on my watch no less.

Her: There is always a risk, yes. But isn't the view worth it?

He stops to think a minute, taking in the streaks of orange
and swirls of light purple across the sky that look like blown glass.
Things look different in that moment. Sharper.
Like someone dialed up the saturation and detail on a photo
and reduced all the noise. He sighs and steps closer,
hoisting himself up and over the wooden railing.

Him: You know, I've worked this route for six years and never
once crossed that fence.

Her: Sometimes it just takes another person to go first. Baby steps.
I think that's what they call progress. Welcome, friend.

Visceral

There is a stirring
a rustling
a shaking
a quivering I cannot fully describe or understand
but it is limbs reaching
arched cathedrals of ravenwood and pine bone
cut from the corners of time
spring and summer in February's final winter

I lean towards it
the entirety of my body buzzing
becoming something other than what it is
and everything of what it is not
all of what it could be

I am a body of questions trying on different sounds
searching seeking
hungry for meaning
anything to offer even the smallest morsel
of what it is to be consumed

This is a Universe based on Expansion

If I could tell you one thing today it would be *try*—
pluck the silver lining from the dying rose,
from the sorrowful song, from the simple poem.
When you pause to inhale the moment, it will materialize as a reflection
of all things great and small and will ask you to tilt your imagination
towards memory, to recall every soft thing you've ever held.
It will wear your suffering smooth, calm your unruly chaos,
carve resounding glory from your stone.
It will take your pain in two palms
and lower it gently into the crooning river,
bury it in a ravine, nourish you with rain's wisdom.
It will grow you and repot you, uproot you and transplant you
in the truth of your own making.
Even thorns become thimbles when stitched with enough perspective.
Gratitude is birthed from ache. Time is a mother's hush
and resilience is treasure unearthed from your greatest challenge.
Your potential is the clashing symbols of starry-eyed expansion.
Your soul traverses infinite possibilities, gathering knowledge
like a bouquet of rogue wildflowers growing
where no one said they would grow, wanting
to know itself, *to name itself*.
If I could tell you one thing today
it would be to pry your chest cavity a little bit wider,
hold it open a little bit longer.
With enough time and only the tiniest bit of love,
everything silver turns to gold.

I Spy gets a Glow-Up

I spy with my little eye something...*red*
red raspberry
berry-stained palms
palm fronds, ferns, and evergreen words
words that grow gardens
garden of Eden
Eden and Eve
eve of takeoff
taking off from sky into love spread wide
widened view
view from the bottom

bottoms up
up up and away
away or towards
towards is forward
forward motion turbine turning
turning the clock hands
hands to hold
holding hearts
heart meets mind
the mind sees what the heart believes

believe it to be so
and so it is
is it a red raspberry I spy?

no
I spy with my little eye
passion, possibility
a purposeful life

For those who never read the instructions

Don't get up too early. I know you have this thing and that thing and you're all about the doing and the going and the trying-to-get-to-work-by-nine, but you also have that special kind of morning light that only shows up at a certain time and a person beside you that might not always be around. Hold that person a little longer. A little tighter. Tell them you love them. Tell them again three different ways in the same day. Give thanks.

Have an extra cup of coffee. Set the alarm a bit earlier so you can sip in peace on the back deck. On rainy days, hit snooze. Three times. Roll over and be the big spoon. Give thanks. Drive with the windows down. Get messy. Put your hands in earth, in dough, in paint. Offer things to those in need: money, time, love. Give thanks.

Spend the extra money for organic vegetables. Cook more often. Together. Make your plate a rainbow with red and yellow pepper and avocado. Give thanks. Tell the absolute *dumbest* jokes. They will make you laugh the hardest. Read more books and put down the phone. Star gaze. Eye gaze. Say goodnight in a foreign language. Make it fun. Switch it up. Give thanks.

Point out every animal-shaped cloud. Be spontaneous and visit a nearby small town. Get lost and see where you end up. Swim naked in a river. Nap in the sun. Give thanks. Fall in love more than once. Give your heart to every flower, every tear, every stranger just asking for an ear. Give thanks. Indulge your senses. Eat. Experience. Embrace. Give thanks.

Never stop learning. Give thanks. Tell yourself, "I love you" and acknowledge the awe that is your life. Give thanks. Write your own instructions. Put them in a safe place.

When you forget, give thanks.

As Told

Dreams, emotion, love
they will guide you into golden
make you skilled at this game
attuned to its tricks so that everywhere
is sanctuary; everything
has purpose.

you learn the rules.
you break them.
you make this life your own.

Goodnight

What makes a good night?

When we say it, do we mean,
"I have made it to the end of this day,
the unspooling of time has lead me here,"
and sometimes here is a wonderful place—
shoes at the door, a small but tidy apartment
with a kitchen window box,
someone waiting up in the living room,
brightening as you walk in.

Or here,
the empty box of plaster and drywall,
the dirty dishes still in the sink,
the piles of clothes on the floor
you wish were someone else's
as the notifications ping in your jeans' pocket.

In either scene, there is a smile.
One on a face, one coming through a screen.
There is a moon and a sky and love.
The night is good.

Now a little help for my friends, the ones I know and the ones I haven't met

Words are such a gift.
Breath is such a gift.
To be you is such a gift.

Promise me you won't squander it. This life, all of it.

Before you even came here, you looked down from the musical accompaniment of stars in the cascading infinite, smiled, picked Earth and said, *"This.* This is the one." Despite strife, hardship, differences, you keep creating *as you are being created.* It is only ever you that holds out a waiting hand for your own acceptance.

Take it.

No one will ever again, in the history of this world or the next, look, laugh, or love in the way that you do. No one will think exactly like you or know the things that you know, see the way that you see, exist in the way that you exist.

Not a single being.

Ever.

You are a rare book, indeed. A classic timeless and beloved story. A once in a lifetime event. A firework glimpsed from the windowsill off in the distance. The exact arrangement of amber and gold flecked clouds scattered along a sunset. How can you not see that? *Friend,* it is you!

Do not take this life for granted, in all its challenges. Rise to them. Make the difficult, beautiful. Make the unbelievable, true. Find whatever modicum of light you can and push through because this is it. "The One" is you.

As we grow, we gather. We are but this grand gathering of sound, of moments, of emotions. We are gifted as we are given. And one day we will be gone but the ideas stay behind. How you lived stays behind. What you turned to glory stays behind and it lives on and on in everyone you have ever touched, everyone you have ever loved. You are already enough, as you are, here in this very moment, and the flaws you see are only your perception as experienced from this precise blip of time, with your current state of mind. If you don't see something you like, it can and will change. You can always be rearranged. Shapeshifter, heart lifter, light bringer, you are all of it and then some. **You won't ever happen again.**

I am sold on you.
I am pulling for you.
I am holding out for you.

If we are what we love, then let me love you. If we are what we love, then take hope, take possibility, take change and become. If we are what we love, then love from a room with a view, punch holes in the walls, rip down the roof. Keep choosing this life and build something new.

I believe body, mind and soul in the truth and *friend*...
...the truth I believe in is you.

But what does it all mean?

It's the way the morning light looks so *unbothered*
like a grandmother's deep laugh lines,
these traces of Michelangelo's David along her skin
and the intrinsic wonder-world of the infinite within
it's a chair slowly pushed back from the table in a quiet room,
scraping and screeching against the floor, saying
"it's my turn to speak" it's buying birthday cake
for your own birthday and bringing it to the party
so your friends won't go hungry it's the good ship lollipop
and a sucker punch through teeth
decaying from too many sweet nothings that tasted sour
it's the Quiet Ones beginning to molt, shedding skin to become
the women of the hour stacked on the continuance of forever
because we stretched before this, we're limber, we're loose
it's being so used to the way the world
pressed us against a wall with his knife to our throats
that it took seeing the stringy guts of soul
and its counterpart shadow in red eyes and a growl
to carry us back up and make our way out.

It's a pen shoved in our hands asking us to once again
write ourselves out of the problem it's a scribble and a scratch
that was more than noteworthy, more than post-its,
more than pages because *these words*...
can't be contained it's aching to be free
each piece a strip that says TAKE ONE
hung publicly for all to see
it's flagging down that monster truck thought
so you can hitch a ride down the 405 through hell

and arrive on a stage to tell the tale
of how you bloodied both knees on the concrete
trying to climb inside.

It's passing the blunt message around
and filling the room with raspberry smoke
but removing all the mirrors
so everyone else can see a little clearer when it all settles
it's putting on the good lingerie, the one he appreciates
and crying when he notices **you** instead of just the lace
and you feel like a gold medal, a gold star, and the five golden rings
from the song after years of society's hand feeding you
that you were absolutely right to bite.

It's the world turning on a spotlight
after too long of monsters under the bed
from the haunted rooms inside your head
it's the music you're making with a pen
it's the rising from the dead for the third time
it's a soul story and ten thousand boisterous songs
it's not throwing away the smallest one that got left behind because…
you're learning about recycling.

It's paper mâché Tuesdays while everyone else paints
it's the determination of doing this shit differently
it's not always making sense
it's a grand slam of scaling the fence
it's choosing paper over rock and scissors
it's making love to time
it's a punctuation tattoo of why

it's a spinning Saturn on skin
reminding of every beautiful, hard lesson
it's the holy hallelujah amen of a lover's kiss
and church of an open armed embrace
the only one you'll set foot in.

It's taking it's claiming it's slaking
your hundred years thirst with a ruby encrusted goblet of ink
it's crying when it's inconvenient and welcoming that
it's being unapologetically "too much"
it's setting the scene
it's burning rules instead of banning books
it's asking for them to take a second look through love's lens
it's the gospel and scripture of understanding and acceptance
it's a spruce truth forest on fire pining for more
it's a novel kind of folklore never heard before
it's wrung-out hearts rinsed cleaned
it's a billion of the write kind of dreams
it's the jet stream of extreme
it's the Zeliska 600 nitro express revolver of your own resounding scream
it's want being equally important as need
it's the hope it all means something
it's the fire and passion and the unshakable steel belief...
that it does.

Cadenza in the Rising Flame

there is a heat in my chest, a bonfire made
there from certain words that emerge from the dry and brittle brush
dusteaters of what was left behind
blaze and buds born in unison that spell the story
of how a once hollow thing
could both burn and bloom at the same time
when everyone else said it simply could not be done

but oh, *we are not everyone*
who else can wield the weight of a wildfire?
a controlled burn that razes the rest to the ground
to unearth the subterranean sound
and still birth a birdsong where no bird has ever lived?

some say
it's the raw material from which love is made
remnants of wishes and miracles not fully formed
others say it's what was left in the wake of smoldering humanity
mixed with a Molotov cocktail of volatile emotion

I say
it's a little of both
the exact second night ceases being night
and must take life in the rough beauty of its own two weathered hands
leading from cracked bone catacombs into the blinding day
of temple ruins and twisting streets in an imaginative mind maze

through violent brush made beautiful only by those
who know what it is to burn

I call it show and tell
I call it reclamation
I call it a homecoming
I call it the Great Song

I call it an awakening to all the places we find god

Beautiful Pursuit

The year is *it doesn't matter.*
The world is flat.
The world is flat only because everyone believes it to be flat.

Except you.
You set out to prove it is round.
You do.

The year is *I'm not going to spoil the surprise.*
Magic isn't real.
Magic isn't real only because everyone believes it isn't real.

You set out to prove magic is real.
You do.
Now...*what do you tell them?*

An Acceptance Speech on Behalf of the Full Moon

I can't take credit for any of the words I've said today
not the foxes hunting prey among the skillful wordplay
or the riot of rabbits riddled in the rhyme
or the way a simile smells like cherry notes and tobacco
from oak casks of Italian wine

I can't accept your kindness for the tongue-tied titles
or the mouthwatering metaphors
the ones that leave me ravished and famished
frothing at the mouth for more

not the stunning sapphires
and exquisite emeralds glistening in plain sight
not the tangled fishing line of mind
to see which schools of thought will bite
and certainly not the way I dive for shadows
and coax them towards the light

not the poems made from playlists
or the wise words from a star
not the verbose vernacular of woman
or her subsequent man's repertoire

no, I can't speak to such inspiration
when it came quietly through the night
I just shot the moon into my veins
and then sat down to write

Maverick J. Malone is a writer, poet, and self-proclaimed "unearther of life." She believes in the magic of language as a powerful tool for alchemy, healing, and self-discovery. In 2022, she published her first book of poetry, _Pressed Petals_, chronicling her reclamation and self-love journey. _Hope and Other Beautiful Things_ is her second collection, with a third and fourth both in the works. Currently, she lives in east Tennessee with her young daughter, Lilly.

You can find Maverick on Instagram @mavmalone and on her Substack, _Mentally I'm Here_, at www.maverickmalone.substack.com. You can also check out her podcast, _Ink Speak_, on all major music streaming platforms.

Bonus!

Scan the code below to hear my spoken word piece "Notes to More Than Self" and listen to this book's companion playlist.

Let's keep the magic going.